I Can Write
Letters
and E-mails

Anita Ganeri

Heinemann
LIBRARY
Chicago, Illinois

www.capstonepub.com
Visit our website to find out more information about Heinemann-Raintree books.

To order:
☎ Phone 800-747-4992
🖳 Visit www.capstonepub.com
to browse our catalog and order online.

Edited by Daniel Nunn, Rebecca Rissman, and Sian Smith
Designed by Victoria Allen
Picture research by Elizabeth Alexander
Original illustrations © Capstone Global Library Ltd 2013
Illustrated by Victoria Allen and Darren Lingard
Production by Victoria Fitzgerald

Originated by Capstone Global Library Ltd
Printed and bound in China by Leo Paper Products Ltd

Hardback ISBN: 978 1 4329 6935 6
Paperback ISBN: 978 1 4329 6942 4

16 15 14 13 12
10 9 8 7 6 5 4 3 2 1

Library of Congress Cataloging-in-Publication Data
Cataloging-in-Publication data is available at the Library of Congress.

Acknowledgments
We would like to thank the following for permission to reproduce photographs and artworks: Alamy pp. 7 (© Jack Sullivan), 24 (© imagebroker), 25 (© Caro); Corbis p. 5 (© Renee Lynn); Shutterstock pp. 4 (© Darrin Henry), 6 (© KariDesign), 7 (© Goodluz), 8 (© notkoo), 9 (© EDHAR), 10 (© Feng Yu), 10 (© Vishnevskiy Vasily), 10 (© Chas), 11 (© Elena Schweitzer), 12 (© PeJo), 15 (© Ramona Heim), 17 (© Lorelyn Medina), 17 (© gladcov), 18 (© photosync), 19 (© lev dolgachov), 20 (© Selyutina Olga), 21 (© mattasbestos), 23 (© 75621280), 26 (© fusebulb), 27 (© iadams), 27 (© PePl).

Every effort has been made to contact copyright holders of material reproduced in this book. Any omissions will be rectified in subsequent printings if notice is given to the publisher.

Disclaimer
All the Internet addresses (URLs) given in this book were valid at the time of going to press. However, due to the dynamic nature of the Internet, some addresses may have changed, or sites may have changed or ceased to exist since publication. While the author and publisher regret any inconvenience this may cause readers, no responsibility for any such changes can be accepted by either the author or the publisher.

Contents

What Is Writing? 4

What Are Letters? 6

Different Letters 8

Writing Style 10

Laying Out a Letter 12

Starting and Ending 14

Letter to a Pen Pal 16

Thank-You Letter 18

Formal Letter 20

Sending a Postcard 22

How E-mail Works 24

Writing an E-mail .26

Top Tips for Writing Letters and E-mails 28

Glossary 30

Find Out More 31

Index 32

Some words are shown in bold, **like this**. You can find out what they mean in the glossary on page 30.

What Is Writing?

When you put words on paper or on a computer screen, you are writing. It is important to be able to write clearly so that readers can understand what you mean.

What do you like to write about?

Letters are delivered to your door.

There are many different types of writing. This book is about letters. Letters are a type of **nonfiction**. This means that they are about facts and real life.

What Are Letters?

A letter sends its reader a message or tells him or her some information. The writer puts the letter in an envelope and sends it in the mail.

We put stamps on letters so that we can mail them.

People on vacation send postcards.

Sending an e-mail is quick and easy.

Other ways of sending a message are to write a postcard or **e-mail**. An e-mail is a type of letter that you write on a computer. Then you send it to the reader's computer.

Different Letters

There are lots of different types of letters. People write letters to say thank you, invite someone to a party, tell someone some important news, or just catch up with friends.

Party invitations are fun to write.

You are invited to my party on August 20 at 5:00 p.m. Please come to 7 Park Road, Spring Green.

A job application needs to be neat and clear.

People also write letters to apply for jobs or to complain when something goes wrong. Sometimes it is quicker to write an **e-mail** instead.

Writing Style

When you are writing a letter, think about the person you are writing to. If you are writing to someone you do not know, use a **formal** style of writing.

Use polite language, like "I would" when you are writing a formal letter.

Dear Mr. Fisher,

I would like to

become a member of

your bird-watching club...

If you are writing to someone you know, use a more **informal**, chatty style of writing. Always make sure that your writing is clear and easy to understand.

Use chatty language, like "thanks" when you are writing an informal letter.

Dear Aunt Jan,
Thanks for my great
present. I love it!

# Laying Out a Letter

It is important to set your letter up in the right way. This makes it easier to understand. On the opposite page, you can see how to **lay out** a **formal** letter. How to write an **address** on an envelope is shown below.

Mrs. Jones
The Supermarket
10 Brook Street
Chicago, IL 60614

Reader's address at top left

Your address at top right

**7 Oak Street
Chicago, IL 60612**

**The Supermarket
10 Brook Street
Chicago, IL 60614**

May 12, 2012

Greeting

Date underneath

Dear Mrs. Jones,

I am writing to complain about the bananas I bought from your store last week. They were very soft and brown. They tasted horrible.

I look forward to hearing from you.

**Sincerely,
Jack Walton**

Signing off

Starting and Ending

There are different ways to start and end letters. Here, you can see how to start and end a **formal** letter to someone you do not know.

Dear Sir or Madam,

Sincerely,

If you don't know the person's name, say, "Dear Sir or Madam."

Dear (person's name),

Sincerely,

You can sign formal letters with "Sincerely."

Here, you can see how to start and end an **informal** letter to someone you know well.

Dear (person's name),

Best wishes/Love,

Use "best wishes" or "Love" if you know the person really well.

Letter to a Pen Pal

Imagine that you are writing a letter to a **pen pal**. You are writing to make friends. You may have never met your pen pal, but you can still make your letter chatty.

Make your letter **informal** and friendly. You do not need to write the other person's **address** in an informal letter.

13 Apple Street
Smyrna, GA 30080

September 5, 2012

Dear Gabriela,

How are you? I am your new pen pal. My name is Lucy.

Think about what to say in your letter. Your pen pal may live in another country. His or her life may be very different from yours.

Here are some things you might want to tell your pen pal. Ask the pen pal questions, too.

Things to write about

- **yourself**
- **your family**
- **your pets**
- **your school**
- **your hobbies**

Thank-You Letter

Try writing a letter to thank your aunt for your birthday present. Start off your letter by saying why you are writing and why you like the present.

A thank-you letter can be chatty and **informal**.

Dear Aunt Liz,
Thank you very much for the cool crayons you sent me for my birthday. They were just what I wanted...

Sometimes you might have to say thank you for a present you did not like! How can you be polite about it? Here are some words to help you describe the present.

Can you think of any more useful words?

Useful words

interesting

unusual

surprising

kind

fascinating

Formal Letter

You are writing a **formal** letter to your local zoo. You want the zoo to help you with a school project. Plan what you are going to say before you start writing.

Useful tips

- **Explain why you are writing.**
- **Explain how they can help you.**
- **Thank them for reading your letter.**
- **Use the correct beginning and ending.**

You might want to enclose a **SASE** (self-**addressed**, stamped envelope) with your letter. Write your own address on the envelope and stick on a stamp.

An SASE is useful if you want people to reply. It saves them the trouble of finding an envelope or buying a stamp.

Holly Alston
Ashfields School
Santa Clara, CA 95050

Sending a Postcard

People often write postcards when they go on vacation. You write your short message on the left-hand side. You write the reader's **address** on the right-hand side.

Make sure that you leave room for the address.

Hi there!

Having a great time. Hotel is amazing, with huge pool. Going surfing tomorrow. Wish you were here. See you soon!

Love, Asif

Charlie Parker
1 Manley Road
Cleveland, OH
44101

You can write a postcard in an **informal** way. There is not much space on a postcard, so you can leave out your address and a greeting.

Things you might say

- **where you are**
- **what you have been doing**
- **what the weather is like**

Here are a few things you could say.

How E-mail Works

An **e-mail** is a letter or note that you send on a computer. "E-mail" is short for "electronic mail." An e-mail is very quick and easy to send.

Writing an e-mail is a quick way to send a message.

To send an e-mail to someone, type in his or her **e-mail address**. Then write your message and press "send." Press "reply" to answer an e-mail that someone has sent you.

Always read an e-mail again before sending it. Once you click "send," it is too late to change it!

Writing an E-mail

Like letters, **e-mails** can be **formal** or **informal**. Begin a formal e-mail with "Dear…" and end it with "Sincerely."

The date appears **automatically** in the e-mail.

To: D.Robinson@Museum.com
Subject: School trip
Date: Wed, Oct. 24, 2012

Dear Miss Robinson,

We really enjoyed our visit to your museum last week. Thank you for guiding us.

Sincerely,

Izzy Price

E-mails to friends are informal and chatty. You can write them in note form. You can start them with "Hi" and end them with "Love" or "See you soon."

An informal e-mail is like a note.

To: Joe6@no.address.com
Subject: Party
Date: Fri, Nov. 16, 2012

Hi Joe!

Party tomorrow afternoon— can you come?

See you soon,

Luke

Top Tips for Writing Letters and E-mails

1. If you are writing a **formal** letter, make sure that your handwriting is neat and easy to read. You can also write it on a computer.

2. Read through your letter or **e-mail** before you send it. Check your spelling and correct anything that is wrong.

3. Keep your **sentences** short in a letter, especially if it is to someone you do not know. This makes it easy to read and understand.

4. Before you write your letter, make a quick note of what you want to say.

This is especially useful if you are writing a letter to complain about something.

5. Write your letter on ruled, or lined, paper. This will help to keep your writing in straight lines and make your letter look neater.

6. When you are replying to a letter, write a rough copy, or draft, first. Make sure that you answer any points or questions in the letter.

7. If you see the letters "RSVP" on an invitation, it means "please reply." This will help the sender to plan the party.

8. Keep practicing! Writing is like playing tennis or basketball. You need to keep practicing.

Glossary

address where a person lives, including the house number, street name, city or town, and zip code

automatically without you having to do anything

e-mail letter that you write and send on a computer. "E-mail" is short for "electronic mail."

e-mail address address you use when you want to send someone an e-mail

formal language that is correct and follows the rules

informal language that is more friendly and breaks some of the rules

lay out to set out a letter on a piece of paper in a clear way

nonfiction writing that is about real people or things

pen pal friend you write to, even though you may never have met the person

SASE self-addressed, stamped envelope. This is an envelope with your own address on it and a stamp.

sentence group of words that makes sense on its own

Find Out More

Books

Ganeri, Anita. *Getting to Grips with Grammar* series. Chicago: Heinemann Library, 2012.

Warren, Celia. *How to Write Letters and E-mails* (How to Write). Laguna Hills, Calif.: QEB, 2007.

Internet Sites

Facthound offers a safe, fun way to find Internet sites related to this book. All of the sites on Facthound have been researched by our staff.

Here's all you do:

Visit www.facthound.com

Type in this code: 9781432969356

Index

addresses 12, 13, 16, 21, 22, 23, 25
automatic dating 26

chatty language 11, 16, 18, 27
complaint letters 9, 29
computers 7, 24, 28

dates 13, 26

e-mail addresses 25
e-mails 7, 9, 24–27, 28
ending e-mail and letters 14–15
envelopes 6, 12, 21

formal style 10, 13, 14, 20–21, 26, 28

greetings 13, 14, 15, 23, 26, 27

handwriting 28

informal style 11, 15, 16, 19, 23, 27

job applications 9

laying out a letter 12–13
letters 5, 6, 8–23, 28–29

nonfiction 5

party invitations 8, 29
pen pals 16–17
polite language 10, 19
postcards 7, 22–23
practicing 29

rough drafts 29
RSVP 29

SASE (self-addressed, stamped envelope) 21
sentences 28
signing off 13, 14, 15, 26, 27
spelling 28
stamps 6, 21
starting e-mails and letters 14–15

thank-you letters 8, 18–19
top tips 28–29

writing (what it is) 4
writing paper 29
writing style 10–11